Fanny

A Cook's Tale

James Wood

Fanny

A Cook's Tale

Piculet

2018

Piculet Press books can be ordered
through Amazon
from other online booksellers
or through bookstores.

CATALOGING DATA
Wood, James.
Fanny: A Cook's Tale / by James Wood. – 1st ed.

1. Family Dynamics — Generational 2. Social Life and Customs
3. Country Estate 4. Murder/Suicide
5. Poetry—Dramatic Narrative 6. Dramatic Monologue

BOOK DESIGN BY
John Balkwill / Lumino Press

AUTHOR'S NOTE

Fanny is a dramatic narrative in free verse set in a mansion on an estate in the country.

If a book of poetry makes you feel like you've opened the door to the wrong room, hang on. Come on in and poke around. Poetry has the power to communicate emotion and tell a story that no other form has.

It's teatime for Fanny, the longtime cook at the Estate. She's just put on a big luncheon for Mrs. P and her houseguests who have gone on to a large wedding on a neighboring estate.

As she rests and waits for them to return she thinks about her life on the Estate and people she's known there—the dowagers, Mrs. P and Mrs. L, who have been friends and closet competitors since childhood; Cammie, Mrs. P's adult daughter who is "not right"; My George, Fanny's boyfriend, who owns the little garage and filling station out on High Road; and her friend Gertie, the cook at Parson Baker's estate at the time of the murder/suicide.

The poem flows on Fanny's voice so read it casually like a letter, novel or a magazine. If it doesn't flow for you, you can always back out and leave as quietly as you came.

My hope is that you will find it interesting and stay on to the end.

"The strength of music is when it makes a personal connection to the listener; when it accesses your own memories and experience. If I, as the composer, say what I am thinking about, it is like stealing from your experience."

LERA AUERBACH

". . .is there any yoked creature without its private opinions?"

GEORGE ELIOT
Middlemarch

Fanny

A Cook's Tale

Teatime Fanny
Personal teatime
Undo apron
Take weight off white orthos
Have a little chat with yourself.
I don't mind if I do.

Fanny

Our big luncheon today
Was a great success
With Mrs. P and our houseguests.
My George teased me about it later
"Well done Fan!" he said,
"But where will it be tomorrow?"
Loves to tease, My George does,
Owns the little garage and gas station
Out on High Road.
Takes care of cars
Valuable trade we all know that
But you can't eat cars.
After our luncheon everyone except
Our Cammie and Mrs. L
Went next door to Weldon Estate
For huge wedding
So now I get to rest a bit.
Manuel's cut my flowers
They're over there
In that old zinc sink
With the 'S' shaped divider
Waiting for my arranging;
Cammie and Mrs. L
Also waiting
In other wing of Our Mansion
For their movie about wedding.
Bad idea if you ask me
Not good for Our Cammie

Not good at all.
For same reason as Mrs. P
Wouldn't let Cammie go
To real wedding this afternoon:
Brings up The Past.
I understand that
But why not let Mrs. L go?
Mrs. P just smiled and
Said, "Oh there isn't any . . .
"There's no room in the carts."
That wasn't so,
There was plenty of room.
All she had to do was
Tell Mr. Sterling to hoist his big butt
And scoot over to let Mrs. L in.
Why didn't she do that?
I do not know
But poor Mrs. L
She caught on fast.
Soon as she heard
"No room in carts"
She sent her bent little body
Back over Upper Lawn into Our Mansion
Quick-step
Like she was caught
In sudden summer storm.
She took it well considering
The blow it was to her:
For our other guests, the Weldon Wedding

Fanny

Is just routine entertainment of a weekend;
In Mrs. L's wee world
It was to be
The Event of her small Season.

And yet
When deprived of it
She moved right on
Or seemed to.
Back in Our Library she says,
"This is so exciting
"I can't wait to see that lovely movie
"Bing Crosby and beautiful Grace Kelly
"I'll never forgive myself if we miss it,
"Old movies bring everything back."
She's right about that
Old movies, old tunes
Do dredge up The Past,
Forgotten dreams and hopes
Come swarming
Bringing old selves,
Those we loved and
Those we didn't.
Then she says,
"It's so sad about Poor Thing."
"Poor Thing" is what she calls
Princess Grace.
"Poor Thing's life was ruined
"By her social-climbing parents

"And that Catholic Church,
"Pushing her to marry
"That fancy foreigner.
"Real King, I guess
"But what a puny throne
"For famous movie star!"
Ha, ha.
Mrs. L is funny
Very funny.
Still
None should laugh at age.
No
Age strips us bare.
Of course with Mrs. L
It's sometimes hard to tell
What's age and what's
Just Old Mrs. L shining through,
She was always hard to fit
In the fridge.
One thing for sure
Like I said
Not good for Our Cammie
Watching movie wedding.
Risky, very risky
Never know what might catch fire
In that memory bin.
We've been so careful for so long,
Never letting out a whisper
Our Cammie might pick up

Fanny

And she's over thirty now.
Can it have been that long?
Oh yes
Years have passed
So many years
And Mrs. L's thermostat is showing it.
In The Library she says
"Fanny,
"Shouldn't we light that beautiful fire?"
Then to Cammie
"Wouldn't that be cozy ?"
Cammie stays silent
Keeps on with her cards
Wearing that tight-lipped little smile
She's been using lately,
Smile that tells you nothing.
Fact is
This time of year
We don't need fire
Plenty warm without it.
But old folks always cold
And love staring at fires.
Fires do bewitch
It's true
I'll give 'em that.
Look at a fire
In a fireplace I mean
Not forest fires or wildfires
God forbid a house fire

But really look at fire
And soon you're in another world.
You see what children see:
Fiery tongues
Licking the logs away
Red hot bits of bark
Like ruddy ice cubes
Crashing softly
Into beds of glowing ash.
Stare at a fire
And fireplace becomes theater
Exotic worlds on parade
Entire civilizations passing by
While passing on.
With that in mind,
For Mrs. L's fascination
And warmth,
I light the fire.

Then,
The others gone
I go to Living Room
To tidy up
Plump sofa cushions
Brush cracker crumbs
From oval marble tops
Of tiny tables,
Thin fluted legs
Resting in the rubble

Fanny

Of the Stilton.
And as I do
I hear Mrs. L in Our Library
Say something to Cammie about
"Your sister's wedding"
And "back then."
She shouldn't be talking
About weddings
Not to Cammie,
Not about a wedding "back then."
Mrs. L should know but
Maybe she just forgot.
Later
Looking out the kitchen window
I see Cammie start her
Regular little walk around
Our big old Rose Garden.
That tells me Mrs. L
Is left alone in Library
So I should make my move.
I shoot over there to warn her,
Remind her to avoid certain topics
With Our Cammie.
Good idea
But did not work.
Mrs. L greets me with a smile
I start to speak
Then right away
She waves me off

Starts acting very strange
As if she doesn't understand.
Is it her age again?
Hard of hearing?
Who knows?
She's Mrs. P's best friend, but she's
Always been a strange case
Kind of a shape shifter.
She might be hearing fine
Just pretending she can't
Because she disagrees,
Disapproves
Or her mind
Has taken French leave.
I don't know.
But I can't let it go at that
This is too important.
I keep talking
Louder
Telling her to be careful,
Not to mention weddings
To Our Cammie.
Now I'm almost yelling
But Mrs. L is worsening
Scrunching up her face
Hands fluttering
Like frightened birds in cage
She can't sit still
Bobbing about in chair.

Fanny

That's when
I get queasy feeling,
Am I missing something?
I turn around
And yes I am,
It's Cammie.
She's come into the library
Behind my back
Cut short her walk
Or I lost track of time.
When did she return?
What did she hear?
Me?
Talking about her and Her Harvey?
Or when she was maid of honor
At her sister's wedding?
Don't know
I do not know
Silently, suddenly
She was there
Sitting at her little table
Playing her solitaire
Wearing her po face.
When Cammie plays solitaire
She never gets excited
Not for winning
Not for losing.
Is it her pills?
I don't know but

Deadpan she is
Like she's entranced or
In a bad dream,
Stirring an endless pot.
Makes all the right moves
Turn three and build down
Aces to top of board
Build up there.
Moving slowly
Everything done proper
And just the same
For all these years.
It's a mystery
She's a mystery
A lovely sad mystery . . .

C'mon Fanny, quit stewing!
Get a grip!
Forget all that.
It's Teatime
Fanny's Hour.
Time to ponder Big Questions:
Like,
"What will happen to Fanny
"When this job is gone?"
Nothing goes on forever
Things here are changing around.
No more Big Staff
Just sometimes Rent-A-Help

Fanny

Everyone's getting old
Old hands are dropping off
Even Gifford.
Oh yes
Gifford-the-Butler
Plucked from life
While straining on his porcelain throne.
Whisked off its varnished seat
Like big old housefly.
Mrs. P never got new model
Of Gifford
Nor of Mr. P after he passed.
Maybe she thought, "Free at last!"
But she'd always ruled roost anyway.
You can't push her around
Not that Mr. P ever tried.
Oh no,
When sky got dark
He'd leave for Office
Or his Club.
Mrs. P is one strong lady
Strength born of neglect I say
Childhood neglect.
Children of rich families . . .
What people forget is . . .
They forget wealth can be gilded ghetto.
Poor-little-rich-girl stuff no joke
Not for Mrs. P anyway
She had to teach herself

How to survive
And she did.
Money didn't spoil her
No
She's down to earth
Got it from us I think
From Staff,
Specially Old Cook and me,
We kind of raised her.
She's glad to chat with us,
Despite our moving in separate circles.
Old Cook used to tell
About one evening,
Long ago it was.
After a big dinner party
The guests gone home
Mrs. P comes out
To Butler's Pantry to thank Staff.
Everything cleaned up
Dishes put away
Behind glass doors
Of cabinets over counters,
Flannel separators between dishes
Cups hanging on hooks
Above their saucers
Flatware washed and dried
Each piece back in the sleeve
Of its own flannel flap bag
Bags lying flat

In shallow drawers.
But one part of Our Butler's Pantry
Still beautifully messy
Petals and stems
Thorns and leaves
Scattered on countertops
Where Old Cook is arranging flowers
Like I do now.
Flowers for next morning,
The Breakfast Room
Guest rooms and landings
Tables in long upstairs halls.
Standing there in Butler's Pantry
Mrs. P picks up rose petals
Crushes them and
Sniffs her fingers.
Then she gets dreamy look
And says
"I have a pillow filled with petals."
"You do?" from Old Cook.
"Petals from the flowers
"My admirers gave me."
"Oh I see" says Old Cook
Keeping on with her flower arranging.
"One from each of my beaus"
Says Mrs. P,
"Seven, seven big bouquets."
"My goodness!"
"Oh Yes,

"Seven beaux."
"You had seven?"
"Yes, not counting the one
"Who became Mr. Pearce."
"Good Heavens," says Old Cook
"And I saved those bouquets.
"Until the petals dried
"Light as feathers.
"And even dried
"They still kept their sweet scent.
"I couldn't bear to throw them out."
"No," says Old Cook.
"So I asked Ilse, our seamstress,
"To fill a pillow with them
"And Ilse did.
"Then,
"When I married Mr. P
"I knelt on it,
"Knelt on my petal pillow filled
"With the remains of my seven suitors'
"Attempts to win my hand."
Old Cook said that was "symbolic"
"Pure symbolic."
In fact,
When it came to kneeling
Old Cook and me
We saw Mrs. P do that
From time to time
On Mr. P

Fanny

In a genteel way of course,
Only enough to stay in shape
And keep things understood.
She's always attracted men
Even today men send flowers. . .
But she's not ordering
Pillows.

That long-ago conversation with Old Cook
Is just like Mrs. P,
Even today
She's easy to chat up.
Of course you have to know
Where fences are.
She'll act like it's equals
Probably believes that's so
But risk is yours.
Say the wrong thing
She can switch levels
Quick as a cat.
Then there she is
At top of fence
Eyes on fire
Ready to leap.
Not from meanness
Just to keep things straight
As she understands them.
Old Cook used' to say that
Mrs. P grew up as

"A little pea in empty pod,"
An only child in a huge house.
Mother
Ran off to Argentine
With world-famous polo player
And was lost to her forever.
Father
Rich and handsome
Always away
Never at home
Even when he was.
So she had to decode
Life on her own
Grownups, Society, the World.
Learn how to float
On stormy seas
Amid money, manners and adult mysteries.
Remembering always to be careful
Of grown-ups with long knives,
Long arms, busy hands
Scary zombies with designs.
Then as she blossomed
She had to bear with grace
Everyone requiring
Most pressingly
This or that
She could not
Or would not give.
No, no,

Fanny

I say
Mrs. P's done well
To have survived and be
As kindly meant as she is now.
A bit peculiar perhaps
Due to background
Money and the rest.

Sometimes
She's put me to the test.
The Christmas
After Old Cook passed on
She gave me an envelope
With four big bills.
Later when I thanked Mr. P
He said, "Fanny you are welcome.
 "I hope you put it in the pot
"Where you save for something special."
"Oh yes we will, " I said.
"Four hundred dollars!"
Thinking of the trip in Phaeton
That George and I
Planned for our vacation.
But on hearing "four "
Mr. P had turned away
And murmured to himself,
"It was supposed to be 500 . . . "
When I told George he laughed,
"She lifted one bill for herself

"Thinking no one would ever know."
It angered me at first
Then I remembered Old Cook on
The rich and how they could
Sometimes play Scrooge.
Mrs. P's trick was cheap and small
But could be understood.
When she was young
She was kept outside the wicket
Money was a mystery.
So when she began to get some—
A check from bank or lawyer or trustee—
It went into her shoe.
She learned to hoard
What she received
And to not be picky
About the means by which
It might be made to grow.
If the usher should nod
While passing the collection plate,
Who was she to shun Opportunity?
So I came to see it likely
That she had shaved
Our Christmas gift
Without a qualm
Like I might swat a fly.
That was disappointing
But little harm was done
To me and George.

Fanny

The four bills floated Phaeton
Handsomely on our Vacation.
With all Mrs. P's quirks
Still fond of her I am.
Wouldn't be here if I wasn't.
Brave words Fanny
Where else?

Good, we've arrived
At favorite tea-time topic.
Question of All Questions:
Fanny's Fate:
What happens to Fanny
When Mrs. P is gone?
C'mon, don't fret
You'll slide into good job somewhere
Just on your crème brûlée alone. . . .
Perhaps . . .
But the demand for crème brûlée
Is dropping off
Even out here where Rich Bees live,
What's left of them after The Crash.
True but can't be helped.
So until the fat lady sings
This house My Home
And when the curtain falls
Of course I'll leave the stage.
I came to cook
Not to cry.

So I'll survive by catering
Or take my toque,
To the City where I might write
A play about my life:
"Feeding the Gentry In the Sticks, "
In Four Acts, by Fanny
Heh, heh . . .

Till then I like it here
My George is here
And dirt
The good earth
That makes things grow.
Nature
No crowds.
Space, trees, flowers, birds
Squirrels and crazy raccoons.
Meadows, grass, blue skies
And so we don't forget,
Sometimes dark clouds
Thunder, lightning, and storms.
Sudden excitements too,
When My Cat Serious catches things
Or when strange dogs chase Serious.
Fires and floods
Human stuff too
Some of it good
And some of it not
Just like in the City.

Fanny

We even have murder out here
Oh yes, murder
Not confined to tabloid classes either
Society Page people too.
So sure
I could take my cooking
Right back to the City
Yes I could.
But why?
I like living here with
Mrs. P and Cammie
My George, My Cat Serious.
It's beautiful too and
Look of the land
Reminds me of the Old Country
When I was very young.
And I'm all for the Old Country
As long as they don't send me back.
Here
I have two rooms
All my own in Our Mansion
Two nice light rooms
Good TV too.
So simmer down Fanny
Keep floating down River of Life
In little walnut shell. . . .
Sounds good
But remember
Not sixteen anymore.

Now the river runs
Straight for the falls.
Someday
Mrs. P must hail
The Celestial Cab.
She can't last forever
Despite her being sure she will.
Then with her kin
She will lie down
In the vault on Our Back Forty.
And that will be
When the soufflé
Slumps for us.

What then Cookie?
When Mrs. P is gone
Jobs will vanish too,
Our World will be a memory.
"Development" will take the stage
They'll chop us up
Put in houses, streets, curbs, sidewalks
Power poles, sewers, fire plugs.
Goodbye to Our Mansion
They'll tear it down.
Cracker boxes will sprout
Like weeds from Our Good Dirt,
"Booze & A Bite"
Will raise its skirts
Start serving gilded crap

Fanny

Become a tourist trap.
Cops will change too
Goodbye to Sheriff Benny
We'll get a new firehouse
With no dog and
A fire engine that always starts.
Farewell to stately grounds
And oval pools
That march down Our Hillside.
And open fields,
Bridle paths under pines and oaks;
And goodbye to Fanny's dream
Of golden years in the country.
Well, what's to be done?
Life goes on until not.
"Forget it, Fanny!" says My George.
"Dynamite couldn't get
"You out of here,
"You'll stay till everything is gone
"Then you'll go too."
Makes me sound relaxed about it,
Doesn't he?
Well he's probably right.
So long as job is here
I'll keep working.
But fear's here too
Below surface.
Like knowing tooth's gone bad
And must be fixed

JAMES WOOD

I have options of course
I could join my cousin
In her catering business
But it is slow
And will not shine
Perhaps even survive
Until the tide comes in again
And money gushes like before.
Driving by you cannot tell
But gossip in the galley says
Many Stately Mansions
Are barely still afloat on a
Deep and unforgiving sea
Of debt.
Debt? Not Our Rich!
Oh yes
Beneath the mask
They too are scared.
To be honest
Cooking for catering
Is not like working here
For Mrs. P
Not in the least.
Catering out here now
You're mostly serving New Money
Young ones with new money
And no manners.
A life in service
To those who lack manners

Fanny

Is one unhappy life.
For a decent life in service
You need distance
And manners give you distance.
So I haven't jumped on catering,
'Til then
I like it here
This old house
Mrs. P and Cammie
Old Money with Manners.

Of course
Not all Old Money is decent
Even with manners.
Think of Our Parson B
And what he did.
Terrible, terrible
And he entered world
Sucking silver spoon
Beautiful manners too
Up to a point.
We who serve know
Money alone
Large or little
Is no sign or promise
Of anything worthwhile.
Not of brains or savvy
Certainly not of kindness
Or charity.

So I have to admit
My George is right
I'll hang on as long as I can
But not for the money
Or for prospects
Though Mrs. P keeps saying
"Remember Fanny
"You're family too."
Nice of her to say that
But no retirement package there
No,
Saying is not bequeathing.
Besides she's set on being immortal.
Plans to outlive the moon she does
Let alone Fanny.
She's still in charge
Means to stay so
Oh yes
Set on managing everything
And not just here on Our Estate
No, no Life in general.
Life with capital L.
Her friends die of old age
She thinks it's their doctors.
"Fanny, Mary Galbraith's gone
"Passed on last night poor thing
"So bright and funny at
"Altar Guild flower show last month.
"What could have happened to her?"

Fanny

"Well, Mrs. P, really
"Mrs. Galbraith was old
"Big as Our Barn
"Had three heart attacks
"Gulped her cocktails . . ."
But I don't say it.
Death of friend your own age
Sign of what can happen
What will happen.
Even if you are bound and determined
Not to vanish yourself
Death will still come padding
Of a dark night.
If it's a friend or kin
That will get her attention.
But not for long.
When Mr. P passed on
Mrs. P was quiet
But seemed to stay the same.
She said it felt to her
As though he was still there.
No,
Not even death
Bothers her long:
What Mrs. P cannot control
She will ignore.

Just like Trembles
My George's dog.

But when Trembles is ignoring
She starts shaking
Can't help herself.
Mrs. P doesn't shake like Trembles
Of course.
Mrs. P does not shake
Ever.
Trembles' shaking comes as
Part of her Possum Play.
Curtain goes up as My George tells
Trembles to do something dumb.
Pointing under tool shed he'll say,
"There, Trembles, there!"
Trembles knows what's under tool shed
Knows without looking
Cobwebs, occasional spider
Maybe small snake in grass
And possum, resident possum
Which Trembles knows quite well.
So when My George starts this
Trembles always begins to shake
But she keeps playing My George's game
Goes to tool shed
Lays her nipples in the grass
Peers into soupy darkness beneath shed
Where, just as she knew
She's eyeball to eyeball
With the hissing possum creature
Face long as pointed toes

Fanny

On Manuel's new boots,
Possum lips pulled back
Baring pink possum gums
Sporting sharp possum teeth.
Her big old naked rat's tail
Curled over her back
With platoon of pink-skinned infants
Clinging to it like firemen on fire truck
Huge sad eyes
Locked on Trembles.
But dog has no desire
To disturb possum bus
And in a flash
She leaps away from shed.
No trembling now
She's on a Sunday stroll
She sniffs the air
Then drops her nose
To plow the grass
As if she's searching
Old bone perhaps.
That's Trembles playing
"As if "
As if the possum is not there
But possum is.
Possum is always there.
True of life too:
Some things in life
Cannot be wished away

Can't hide 'em from others either
No, not forever.
Death is one of those things
But there are others.

Take daughter of Our House
Take Our Cammie
Mrs. P's born-late not-right child
Waiting
Over there in Our Library
Right now
For her movie wedding.
While Manuel's big springtime fire
Snaps and pops and sails red
Hot sparks over fire screen
Beyond the hearth
To burn black spots in Kermanshah.
You can't steal happiness
From innocents like Cammie
Without it coming out someday
That's what I say.
Even if they're not right
And Our Cammie's definitely not right.
Someday they may catch on
No matter how slick you've been
No matter how odd they seem.
And when they do catch on
It might not be pretty.
Our Cammie, that girl . . .

Fanny

She's no girl now,
None of us is . . .
Point is something's going on with her
Lately she's changing.
Mrs. P chooses not to notice
But you better believe it Mrs. P
Your little girl's not the same.
Where once she was happy and gentle,
Now she's sullen
And won't say why.
Never seen her angry in her life before . . .
She was always a hap . . .
Wait, wait . . .
Not true, not true
How could I forget?
Yes, once before
She was angry like this
But young, younger.
She'd been at Vale of Oaks,
A place for well-to-do people
Who aren't quite right.
That's where she met Harvey
Her Dear One who
Was not quite right either
Of course
But he was well-mannered,
And handsome too.
After release
From Vale of Oaks

They lived with their families and
Saw each other all the time,
Chaperoned of course.
That time for them was like a dream
Warm and familiar and happy
Very different from the cold strict life
At Vale of Oaks.
But
One day
Without warning
Their dream collapsed
When they were forced apart
The way My George splits wood:
Boom!
His sledge hits wedge
Crack!
Log splits in two.
That's how Our Cammie was
Cut off from Her Harvey.
And that's when her tantrums began
With sullenness and rounds
Of naughty acts.
She was angry and wild
Because no one would say
What had happened
To Her Harvey.
First she released Kiri
Her mother's mute canary
Which Lawson her mother's Siamese cat

Fanny

Plucked from the air
Between opened cage door and piano.
Then she threw the huge glass paperweight
With blue dragonfly stuck inside
Through portrait of Mercy Cortright
Her Mother's ancestor from Maine
Making big hole in Miss Cortright's
Flat-as-a-table-top bosom.
She'd hide a shoe
One shoe
From favorite pair of Mother's
Handmade Italian numbers.
We still find orphans from those days
Behind books in the library
In attic steamer trunks.
And worst of all—
Something that made even me angry—
Sometimes she would not eat.
Absolutely would not eat,
Oh just a bite once in a while.
My food!
Our Cammie refusing my food!
But those things were merely naughty
Childish
Not dangerous.
Her not eating was worrying
Still she was not going to starve,
It merely made her less voluptuous.
But when she arrived at matches

She frightened us all.
Brought everything closer to home.
Oh yes
It did.
Can't say I blamed 'em.
Playing with fire out here
Is not a joke.
Not with Our Toy Fire Department.
No
If you hear church bells ringing
Save on Sunday
Or for wedding
Means fire
Serious fire
Something big is burning up
And our Firehouse has become a madhouse
To which volunteers are streaming.
Gardeners, butlers, bartenders
Country club pros, groundskeepers
Occasional sporting landowner
Busybody houseguests
Hopping around
High on community spirit
Grabbing old oilskin coats
Funny-looking helmets
Struggling to pull left boot on right foot.
Fire truck is refusing to start
Hoses fixing to leak
And Woe

Fanny

Our Firehouse Dog
Is letting off mournful howls
From deep inside her dog house
Because she hates church bells
Sirens and fires too
To say nothing of loud
Backfires from old fire truck.
Woe hangs around Firehouse because
She loves firemen
When they aren't being firemen.
Also loves firehouse leftovers.
During that ding-dong pandemonium
You may wonder
If it might be you
What's going to burn up.
Out here odds favor flames
Especially with houses like this.
Wood
It's made of wood
Old wood.
Very beautiful
But ready to explode
Like a dry Christmas tree.
Oh yes,
Our Cammie and matches
Was a dangerous brew
Frightened me
Even loving Our Cammie like I do.
I hate to say it

But when matches put her
Back in the Vale
I was relieved.
And as for her,
Poor thing,
She went back happily
Not knowing what she would
Or would not find.

That morning she waited in My Kitchen
With her little traveling bag
Waiting for Richard-the-Chauffeur
To drive her to the Vale.
Our Cammie was beautiful then
And full of hope.
"Going to Vale of Oaks, Fanny
"Going to see My Harvey."
Smiling she was.
She'd been so hurt
When Harvey disappeared
Vanishing mysteriously
Hurt us too
Old Cook and me
To see her pain.
But Cammie's pain
Never bothered Richard-the-Chauffeur
No
Nothing ever touched
His token heart

Fanny

Certainly not poor Cammie's fate.
For him she was a satisfaction
Material for a charade.
Oh yes
He'd act it out for us
Old Cook and me
His captive audience
At his teatime
In Servants' Dining Room.
He'd sit stirring his tea
And find a way
To mention Our Cammie,
Then suddenly
In a loud voice,
"Sick!"
He'd bray,
"Sick sick sick!
"Sick in the head."
Bong!
Hitting his head with his teaspoon
Which Cook would later boil
Along with his cup and saucer.
"Too much money does it,
"That's what does it.
"Out here with the Rich Bees
"That's what you learn.
"Money leaks into th' blood, it does."
He'd leap up and prance about,
"Mix Blue Blood with too much green

"Whatah ya git?
"Sludge! Ya git sludge!
"Blood and money turns ta sludge.
"Sludge settles
"Settles in tha' brain pan
"Then brain don't run right."
Bong! with his spoon.
Well, little did he know
Little did watch-charm Welshman suspect
Mud and blood were waiting for him
Just down the road.
That night he packed his black valise
His saddle when chauffeuring
Black valise that raised him
To see through the windshield
Touch Bentley's pedals with
His tiny feet.
Valise that also held
His travelling things
Even if he had nothing planned
Because there was a chance,
He said,
Always the chance
He'd get lucky.
Such luck . . .
Seated on his suitcase saddle
He drove the Pearces into the City.
On his return alone
It was a filthy night.

Fanny

Black as bottom
Of cast-iron frying pan
And pouring rain.
Richard-the-Chauffeur paid no mind.
No, no,
Following his usual routine
He high-balled through the storm
Stopping at favorite roadhouses
As he headed for what
He thought would be
His last stop of the night,
The rowdy dangerous "Slyde Inn"
Where he would keep his tryst
With Emily, the towering barmaid
Known as "Wee Em."
But as he drove
His world had changed around.
Slyde Inn and Wee Em,
Now on far side
Of Tucker's Creek,
Were beyond his reach.
The storm had been at work
And the old bridge,
Sluiced downstream by raging waters
Was gone.
Suddenly Richard and Bentley
Were in mid-air.
And in spite of
The winged ornament

On Bentley's brow
The little Welshman's Pegasus
Came down to earth.
By chance My George
Was also coming home that night
And just before Tucker's Creek
Bentley passed him at high speed.
A terrifying sight,
My George said and
One he could not mistake
Nor later lay to rest.
"My God," he said aloud
To his old truck
"There goes the mad
"Pocket Welshman
"Flying like a banshee."
Then,
In the dark and downpour,
As if he'd thrown a switch,
Bentley's taillights winked out.
My George slammed on the brakes
Got out of his old green pickup
And saw Bentley's tire tracks
Going over the edge.
Holding onto a tree
He leaned way out
And peering down
Into the angry dark
He could make out

Fanny

Bentley way below.
Lying in Tucker's Creek
Her lovely front smashed in
Her beautiful body ravaged
By the raging water.
Then, awful, awful . . .
Richard-the-Chauffeur . . .
I did not like him
But I would not
Have wished him this.
When My George clambered down
The scene was sickening,
Almost made him throw up.
There was no way to help
Richard-the-Chauffeur
Too late, too late.
By then no one
Could have done anything
To save the little rider of bangtails.
The poor fool's head
Dangled by bloody strands
On wrong side
Of what he used to call
The windscreen.
It had been the Last Ride
Of Richard-the-Chauffeur.

Old Cook and me
We went to his funeral.

We'd have gone anyway
Out of Laborers' Loyalty
But Pearces made sure all Staff went.
They were there too of course
Despite losing Bentley
And someone to drive her.
Ha, ha
New Widow Jenny,
Wonderful she was
When minister . . .
Who was that penguin anyway?
It wasn't Parson B
He was away
Being chaplain . . .
Or playing golf.
Anyhow
When the clergyman says
"May he rest in peace"
To the closed coffin
Of Richard-the-Chauffeur
New Widow Jenny pipes up
In this loud voice
To no one in particular
"Peace? Peace?
"Well,
 "By Gawd,
"He sartinly never gave me any!"
Stern looks from Pearces
But Old Cook and me

Fanny

We were roaring inside.
Richard-the-Chauffeur never gave
Old Cook nor me
Any peace neither
Specially at teatime
What with his routine about Our Cammie.
"Sure," he'd say
"That's what happened to Miss Camilla
"Mud in the brain pan
"Needs oil change
"Haw, haw, haw
"Can't be done, no sir,
"Missy's stuck with sludge."
Then bong!
Goes his spoon on his own
Soon-to-be-detached head.
Well,
May the little fart rest
As best befits him
But how we hated his routine
Nothing could shut him up!
And when he'd drunk his tea
And left Servants' Dining Room
I'd do my own charade.
God forgive me
I was only a girl then.
Oh yes
I'd copy him
Old Cook would howl with laughter.

"Sick sick sick," I'd chant
Dancing about
Talking like him.
"Here's your spoon,"
Old Cook would say
As I pranced by,
"Sick in the head,"
Pounding my head with spoon,
"Missy's stuck with the sludge."
Then one day
Before Old Cook could warn me
Cammie walked in behind me.
So quiet
Just like today
When she padded into the Library
While I was trying to warn Mrs. L.
Same thing back then
Except it was in Our Kitchen.
By time I saw her
Too late
It was too late.
She must have heard me
Must have seen me prancing about.
I stood there paralyzed
Trying to think what to say
How to explain my stupid doings.
When I looked up she'd vanished
Gone like a ghost.
My silliness hadn't been aimed

Fanny

At her of course
It was aimed at Richard-the-Chauffeur
But she didn't know that.
So that was my last performance
Never did it again
Not funny anymore,
Not at all funny anymore.

Well time passes.
When Our Cammie came home
After second hospital stay
It seemed she'd forgotten
All about Her Harvey.
She was sweet and calm
Took her pills like good girl
So I thought she'd been calmed
By pills and time.
But lately . . .
Oh, she still takes her pills
Lots of times right here after meals
Comes in from dining room
After dinner with family
Gets bottle from kitchen cabinet
Pops 'em in and down they go.
Least I think they go down,
Unless she's tonguing 'em
Spitting 'em out later.
But I don't think so
'Cause usually she stays

Talks to me a little
Tells me about this and that
My Cat Serious or Manuel
Or My George
New blooms in the garden
Things like that
Sometimes a television show.
Still
If pills do go down
They are definitely worn out
Last year's model
Past prime
Lost their magic
Or maybe she's built up resistance.
Something's going on for sure
Because Our Cammie's changed
Not the same girl
Not same person.
I think it's The Past
She's onto something
Most likely about Her Harvey
When he vanished
Gone from her life
Forever.
She knows there's something
About that
She does not know
But everyone else does.
Nothing worse than being

Fanny

Kept in the dark like that.
Cammie's been in the dark
Her entire life
About many things
And she knows it.
After all these years God knows
She knows it.
Now that she's older
She accepts most of that.
But losing your boyfriend
Suddenly, mysteriously
When he's the biggest thing
In your little life . . .
That's a mystery too personal to ignore.
Long ago
When it happened
When Her Harvey stopped calling her
Or coming over
They told her stupid things.
"Don't worry darling,
"It's all for best."
Which showed they knew something
But weren't telling.
Cammie would start crying,
Pleading,
"Please tell me what happened
"To My Harvey?
"Just tell me what happened."
And she'd get no straight answer.

Just more
"I know it's hard for you, Camilla
"But it can't be helped. . . .
"Now why don't you go find
"Cook's Cat?"
Or,
"Why don't we go . . ."
"We" meaning Cammie alone
"Why don't we go look at the new
"Blooms on the Butterfly Rose Bush
"In the Rose Garden."
Talking down to her
Explaining nothing.
That's the sort of thing she's suffered
All her life long.
But like I said,
When she came back
From hospital this time
She never mentioned Her Harvey.
So we began to think
She'd forgotten all about him.
Of course we never talked about him
In front of her,
She knew we wouldn't
Never asked us.
But now
With her being sullen
Knowing her like I do
I can tell she's angry.

Fanny

She tries to hide it but it's there
Smoldering
Like fire in ashes.
I think what's smoldering
Is the memory and the mystery
Of what happened to Her Harvey.
She's got this little picture
Keeps it hidden
But I've seen her peeking at it.
God knows how or where
She's been able to keep it.
They took everything like that away long ago
But they missed this
From the "Vale of Oaks News"
Little four-pager
Published for the "residents"
Like school paper.
She must have seen Harvey's picture
And torn it out.
But it's been so long. . . .
She's had it so long
Why would it wake her up
Now?

Did she overhear Mrs. P say something?
I don't think so
Mrs. P has always been mum
Around Cammie.
And if Mrs. P doesn't want

To let something out
She doesn't
No slips
She stays silent.
Or she becomes the queen of doubletalk
And you can't tell what she's talking about
Even if you give her the subject.
Same with Mrs. L
Over there in Our Library now
Snoozing in front of Manuel's crackling fire.
Those two women
Are queens of confusion.
Slip into special lingo
Quick as a wink.
And always careful what
They say when Cammie's near.
Of course
Cammie might have figured it out
All by herself.
Sometimes those who aren't right
Have strange powers
Surpass us normals.
Or maybe a piece of my pie
Famous gooseberry pie
Unlocked her mind,
That mind it's so easy
To be superior about.
A bite of Fanny's Pie . . .
And Bang!

Fanny

She got the solving vision!
Such things happen!
They happen.
Besides who knows
What she has figured out
Bit by bit
Sitting there saying nothing
Playing her solitaire
Doing her jigsaws
While others jabber on?
Maybe she's been registering
Sifting, sorting, figuring,
Who knows?
But I doubt she got a clue
From anyone here.
Because like I said
Mrs. P has always been careful
Very careful.
And strict with everyone else too
We all know well
Know all-too-well
What can't be said or talked about.
Why would anyone bring it up,
So long ago it was?
Not many left now who
Even knew about it.
Not Mr. P,
Gone long ago.
Old Cook also

God bless her
And she would not
Have let anything slip.
Dr. Benjamin's still around but
He's as generous with his contents
As a bank vault.
Cammie's sister Ashley?
Married to that phony
Italian Count-No-Account
Fortune-Hunting Husband,
Soft hands
And lizard on the prowl.
Living in Europe
They haven't been here for ages.
Morgan Pearce
Sad little brother who
Left so quietly you hardly noticed
Gentle soul passing through.
Lived out there all alone
Down by Stables
In big old drafty Barn
Where he fixed up
Little apartment
With tiny recording studio
Trying to do something
With his musical gifts
Composing, recording music
That no one heard.
Seeing no one,

Fanny

No visitors, no friends.
Never mentioned by family
And all here on the same Estate.
Oh, they were friendly,
Morgan and his family,
No hard feelings
Nothing like that.
They just left him
To live out his sad little life alone
Barely throwing a shadow.
Then
Last fall he got sick;
Dr. Benjamin came a lot
And Morgan did not get better.
Finally on Christmas Day
A big white ambulance
With a huge red plastic
Holiday wreath
Strapped to its grill
Crept silently
Up Our Long Winding Drive
And took Morgan away
To hospital in the City.
We got skimpy reports
He was in surgery
He was out
In again, out again.
Finally they brought him back here
Thin and pale

Shadow of a shadow.
All well
They said
Everything fixed
Just needs to rest
Regain his strength.
So they put him in his
Childhood Room here
In Our Mansion.
Too weak
They said
For his Barn apartment.
But soon
He was falling apart again.
"Insides are dissolving"
They said.
Now what is that,
I ask you?
Whatever it was
It was something
Because shortly
They were sliding
The grey wafer
Of Morgan's sickly self
Back into the white
Red-wreathed ambulance
To send him back to the City
Where
In no time

Fanny

He was dead.
Family told no one
Kept his death a secret
No obit in newspaper
Nothing.
Did they think he was
Recluse so long
That silence was better?
Or maybe easier?
I don't know
But that's what they did.
Dr. Benjamin took care of mortuary
Staff were not given details
We got them anyway, of course
Staff always does.
So his body came home
Once more
This time
To Vault
On Our Back Forty.
And Staff was there
What's left of us.
Parson B said some words
As Morgan was sealed up
And that was that.
Like scary dream it was
Or sad silent movie
No sound
And worst of all

No music.
For all anyone knew
The man might never have
Tip-toed on the grass
Let alone trod the earth
Fingered a keyboard
Composed a note.
Not right
It was not right
People should not
Be treated like that
Even when dead.
Morgan's spirit must be
Out there somewhere
Floating, waiting.
Waiting for what?
I do not know
For something. . . .
What a family!
Give so much to charity
But very odd with their own.
Well it wasn't Morgan
Let something slip to Cammie
He's been gone too long too.
So we're left with
Puzzle of what
Awakened her anger
And mystery of who
Let it slip out,

Fanny

Whatever it was,
If someone did.

Present houseguest
Mrs. L
Mrs. P's best friend
Since they were very young,
Knows all about Cammie
And her sad life. . . .
Just between us
As Mr. P would often say,
Mrs. L herself is no bargain. . . .
"Quelle numero!"
Mr. P would mumble
As he hurried to escape Mrs. L
Before the "girls" commenced
Their klatch.
"Quelle numero!"
Is France, French for
"There's an odd one!"
To be honest
I think Mrs. L's "odd"
Runneth over.
Perhaps Mrs. P doesn't see
The changes in her friend.
Or she gets so lonely,
Or is so bored alone
That she must ring her up
To come visit anyway.

Today Mrs. L came
As always
In Rolls Baby
Her dark blue
You could call it
Deep purple
Rolls Royce.
She cruised up
Our Avenue of Tall Trees
Past lake-sized oval pool
In Lower Meadow
Past the other
Oval pools
That get smaller
As they climb the hillside
To Our Mansion at the top
Mrs. L perched in the back
Under cashmere robe
Of same color as car.
Rolls stops
Chauffeur opens car door . . .
Nothing happens.
Nothing we can see
But we know from past trips that
Mrs. L is thrashing about inside
Gathering up what she
Wants to be clutching
For her arrival
In Our World.

Fanny

Her entrances can be
Most unusual.
Today
As chauffeur holds the door
She struggles to balance . . .
Something . . .
What can it be?
It can't be gift for her hostess
Not gift-wrapped
Not wrapped at all
No
It's a roll of pink toilet paper
That can't be a gift for Mrs. P.
No no
Besides it's opened
An opened roll
And she's trying to palm
A big piece
That's dangling down.
Mrs. P
Standing at the
Front door of Our Mansion
Greets her friend
In a strange stage voice
"Oh welcome Gladys dear. . . .
"How was your trip?
"Why what's that you have there?"
"Oh, I caught a silly little cold
"Irene dear

"It's nothing, just sniffles."
Right away
You know something's odd
Old folks not supposed to
Travel with colds
Especially not to stay
With other old folks.
"Wouldn't you prefer
"Some tissues dear?"
Says Mrs. P.
"No, no, dear,
"I'm used to it now
"I ran out of tissues"
Says Mrs. L giggling.
Lazy loops of pink toilet tissue
Gently falling
To rest on what Manuel calls "DG,"
The crushed brown rock
Of Our Driveway,
Loops that Mrs. L is trying to trap
And stuff into her handbag.
Meanwhile Mrs. P is frozen with . . .
What's it called?
You know . . .
Backstairs delight . . .
Pleasant guilty feeling . . .
Shameful pleasure . . .
Even a certain gaiety . . .
At misfortune befalling another . . .

Fanny

Divorce, debts, death . . .
Car crash . . .
Crutches, crippled, cancer . . .
Fire . . . ?
C'mon Fanny
Mr. P used to say it all the time . . .
Complaining about things on TV
"There they go again
"Playing on the public's feelings of . . . "
Of what?
His word for it . . .
Thrill of terrible things
Happening to others . . .
Mor . . . Mor . . . two words. . .
Morbid!
That's one!
What's the other?
"Morbid" what?
 "Morbid Fass . . .
"Fascination! Got it!
"That's it!
"Morbid Fascination!"
One of Mr. P's favorite sayings.'
I say that's what Mrs. P
Is feeling about her old friend Mrs. L.
And it's not just the spectacle—
Mrs. L and the toilet paper wars—
No, no
Mrs. P can look at Mrs. L

And fall into Morbid Fascination.
Anytime
Her face locks up
Look of amazed child
Jaw drops
Mouth hangs open
Eyes bug out
And she's transfixed
Paralyzed
Like bird by swaying head of snake.
Still as stone is Mrs. P
Struck dumb.
Then
As Mrs. L begins to speak
Mrs. P leans. . .
No! She is pulled!
Pulled forward,
Strains to see
And hear:
Will it be her old friend
Bright Gladys L speaking?
Or the more recent Mrs. L
Whose wiring may be wearing out?
Sometimes
Mrs. L is still sharp
Sharp as ever
And she was always very smart,
Great actress to boot.
Why, if she didn't know something,

Fanny

At a loss for answer,
She would wing it.
You never know what to
Expect from Mrs. L.

Which brings up another
Morbid Fascination question
Arrived at by turning all this around:
What does Mrs. L see?
Does she notice her friend
Feeding on her decay?
Hard,
Very hard to tell
With these old performers.
And be honest Fanny
When it comes to Morbid Fascination
It ain't just Mrs. P has tendencies,
No no
It's us
All know Morbid Fascination.
God save us
All feel it.
Even Fanny.
Yes, even Fanny . . .
Oh perfect, perfect!
"Case in point,"
As Mr. P would say.
Murder
Murder here in Paradise

Murder at Baker Estate
Murder in our larger family.
Terrible terrible!
But fascinating.
At Our Parson B's for God's sake!
Minister, Piskie minister!
Yes, yes,
Elegant, cultured, soft-speaking
Card-carrying Episcopalian minister.
No parish of his own
But didn't need one did he?
Being so rich.
Parish duties would put damper
On travels, society, women . . .
Leisure in which to do good deeds. . . .
Women?
Oh my yes
Women!
Golf too.
Sure
He was excellent golfer.
The man had many sides . . .
And,
If not otherwise engaged,
He'd step up when asked
By Church or those in need.
As for being parson
He had everything
All the necessities

Fanny

Collars, vestments
Training too
Best schools
University, seminary
Social standing, money.
And,
From time to time,
An understanding wife.
He had every priestly routine down pat—
From prayer book to bedroom—
All duck soup to Our Parson B.
No stage fright there
Marriages, funerals, baptisms . . .
Services for Mr. Walter Freeman
Thomas wedding
Blessing of Filetti Garden . . .
Just to pick a few.
Our Parson B
Knew what to do
Whatever the situation
Sacred, social or personal.
He would have done
Our Cammie's wedding too
If that had worked out.
Fact is
He was unofficial
Pearce Family Parson
On call
Would have been live-in

If not for
That beautiful place of his own.
Like I said
I knew the man myself.
Liked him too
Often here for dinner
Or our big Sunday Lunch
Sunday Lunch painted by famous artist
Who was that man? . . .
English . . .
One who stayed forever.
Always wanted poached egg
On his porridge . . .
Thought we'd never get rid of him,
Immortalized Pearces and their guests
In that huge painting called
The Conversation Piece featuring
Pearces and usual boatload of houseguests
Devouring My Sunday Lunch
In our elegant Dining Room
Seated at our long Dining Room table
Parson B right up next to Pearces.
And next to him
The bird he squired around
As soon as rich Wife Number One
Passed on with her cancer. . . .
Can't remember her name
The one before La Ool-tee-mah,
Eyeful of bubbling sex,

Fanny

Musical comedy starlet du jour
Sang like a squeaky door. . . .
One Sunday Lunch
When we were making do
With outside serving help
A callow Rent-A-Waiter
Pours vichyssoise
All over Miss Musical Comedy
While trying to look down her dress.
Outraged, she was about
To whack the boy
Forgetting the setting and her prospects,
When Parson B,
Sedate as the Book of Common Prayer,
Placed his napkin
In her cocked hand
And with another began dabbing
At her gently elsewhere,
Barely keeping straight face.
After brief blasé glances
The other guests returned
To the joys of Fanny's Cooking.

Back then
Parson B was Chaplain somewhere
And when he could get free
He'd be here often.
I was so young
Just starting out.

Summertime
And that man in dinner jacket
Black tie and dancing pumps
Tall, trim and tan
Coal black hair and moustache
Kindly smile
And so graceful
Moved like a dancer he did
Gliding more than walking
Never in a hurry
Calm.
Just to be around him
Was a comfort
Gentle, reassuring
But fun.
Oh yes
Loved to kid me
Was he coming on?
Would he have gone farther?
Hard to tell, hard to tell
But I think yes
I do think yes.
After meals sometimes
He'd come out to kitchen
Thank Staff
Just like Mrs. P might.
Knew all of us
Always chatted with me
Teased me.

Fanny

He'd say,
"Fanny, let me take you
"Away from all of this."
I'd laugh
"But Parson, I like all this"
Or he'd take my hand in the hall,
"Fanny, when will you marry me?"
I'd come right back
"Why, Parson, whenever you ask me."
Little did I know, little did I know.
Oh yes, I'd joke right back
He didn't frighten me
I liked him
He'd come right up
Put his arm round me
Pull me close. . . .
So friendly and gentle
All very proper.
Oh yes
But also exciting
He smelled wonderful too
Shaving lotion I guess
Probably . . .
All that makes me queasy now
But then I didn't mind
No, he was fun.
Sometimes I wanted to say
"Oh get serious, Parson B."
But not to be mean

I did like him so
Handsome and friendly and rich.
Foolish me
But innocent too
How should I know?
And not the only bird beguiled
No no
My God!
When I think how many women
Chased that man in his round collar
And without it . . .
Or anything else for that matter.
I tell myself I was only kidding
And would never have said "yes" to him. . . .
But who knows, who knows?
What if he'd come on really serious?
Could've happened
Sure could've happened
I was dishy in those days.
Of course by then
I'd sort of become part of the family
Too close, too close.
And just about his daughter's age
Though age never seemed to bother him.
But marry me?
No, he really couldn't
I really wouldn't either. . . .
You think not, Fanny,
Think again,

Fanny

What if he'd come on dead serious?
Had me looking at jewels and travel
Fancy cars, good clothes
Minks and sables
Italian shoes,
Now that's something Italians can do
Make shoes.
But wait
Wait a minute
Oh my God of course.
Where would we live?
Think where we'd live!
Some fancy place
He'd have insisted on huge house
And not just "house,"
Houses.
Apartments too
City and country
Here and Europe
Not just Europe but "abroad"
Different countries, different climates.
This winter in Hawaii
Balmy air, warm sea
Flower behind left ear
Spring?
Oh Paris then.
Headquarters of course
Would be right here
His Estate right here.

Remember
We're not living on parson's pittance
He was rich
Old Money plus
Some from his first wife too
Oh yes.
Houses and big staffs
He'd have insisted on big staffs
Each of our places
Staff of its own . . . .
Staff?
Sure!
You should know by now Fanny
Big house takes a large staff
Lots of servants gardeners maids cooks . . .
Cooks?
Hold on Parson!
Cooks?
Me with a cook?!
Imagine!
Ha ha
No no!
I'm The Cook!
But wait a minute
He wouldn't take that.
No no
He'd demand my doing nothing
Absolutely nothing
Just relax by pool while

Fanny

He played his golf.
I don't play golf
Never sat by a pool either,
Well, not my own.
No . . . Yes . . .
Well there you are.
For us it would be
The life of the rich and famous
Swaddled in luxury
Gadding about the globe
Jetting between mansions
Each one crawling with staff. . . .
Oh quit dreaming!
Wouldn't have worked
Would not have worked at all.
Thanks
But no thanks . . .
Never mind your secret side . . .
The idea of me living like that?
My own mansions?
With cooks?
Ha ha, oh no!
But what a dream . . .

Like a movie.
But how could such a charming man . . .
More than charming
More than just a handsome
Woman-chaser, he was

Making it all the more mysterious.
And sometimes truly devoted
To his calling,
Really was like God's ambassador.
And not just to the upper crust
No
Helped ordinary people too
He did
People in trouble and pain and sadness
Comforted them.
We all knew of his kindnesses
Gave his time and solace too
Sometimes money as well
Could be very generous.
Did lots of charitable things
Volunteered when there were
Disasters at home and abroad
Earthquakes and floods
Comforted survivors
Wives of servicemen who
Did not return,
Other family members too no doubt.
Although in general
His sympathies did seem to flow
Most freely toward women,
And himself
Which amounts to the same thing
I guess.
And sports

Fanny

I mentioned golf.
And clothes
He wore beautiful clothes
Cashmere, lots of cashmere
Soft, smooth cashmere,
Sport coats, sweaters,
Made you want to touch him.
Travel of course . . .
All the things that go with high life.
And yes
Sometimes there was extravagance
And a kind of bravado
Like too much cognac
In plum pudding.
But for us here
For me
He was like family.
And you know how that is . . .
After a while you just accept
And let 'em live their lives.
Wise or silly.

Well
We all missed something
Did not see it coming
Blind we were
All those years
Blind.
While he was living his comfortable life

His handsome female-tempting life
With his privilege and money and golf
His kindness and his charm
Something else was going on.
Pressure?
Oh yes, probably pressure
Pressure must have been building
Like forgotten pot left on stove.
What set him off?
What finally blew the lid off?
Was it jealousy?
Not that anyone knew about
His young wife seemed
Loyal and loving.
Who knows?
"Things happen"
As they say,
Meaning sometimes
Things we don't see coming
That were there all the time
Just waiting to make an entrance.
That's how I think it was.
Some part of Parson B
Was waiting for its time.
Long neglected
Rotting, bulging
Getting bigger and bigger
Waiting to explode. . . .
See, I'm a cook

Fanny

Cooks do not believe in miraculous dishes
Tasty puddings that fall from sky
Pies that coast in
Through open kitchen window
From heavenly bakery ready to eat
No!
Earthly stuff goes on first
Fixings and mixings and cooking
Time and heat.
It's the same when things go bad
Stuff and people spoil
For a reason
Neglect, weakness, fear
Specially neglect.
On that terrible final day
The festering blob deep inside
Our Parson B
Must have up and
Swallowed his soul.
Terrible Terrible.
Had he just forgot about it?
Maybe he thought he had it trapped
Trapped in his personal dungeon
Locked up
Where no one could hear it roaring
Threatening to escape
While he covered his ears
Dug in his heels
And braced his back

Against the dungeon door.
Maybe
On that awful morning
He just awoke too weak
To hold the door
And the monster overwhelmed him.
Was it weakness of age?
No strength to pretend anymore
And mask fell off?
I do not know.
Even more confusing . . .
Our Parson was a man of God.
Where was his faith?
And where was God?
Did he pray for strength
To resist his awful plan?
Did he even plan it?
Don't know
I do not know.
Heal thyself Cook and soufflé will rise!
Yes
Examine yourself
Your own bottomless
Indecent curiosity . . .
But curiosity is only human
Isn't it?
Specially about ghastly things?
And what that man did was ghastly
Ghastly

Fanny

Blood and gore
Blood and gore galore
Carnage on biblical scale
Turkey parts with gravy.
In his own home
That gorgeous house
Where he lived with La Ultima
The beautiful limper.
But afterwards terrible here too
Mea culpa, mea culpa
Me, myself
Yes, yes!
Demanded every sickening morsel I did
Lapped it up like pup eating cow pies.
Disgusting
Disgusting I was.

Gertie
My good friend Gertie
Was Cook at Parson Baker's place.
She was having her tea that afternoon
Just like me now.
Having simple restful
Afternoon Tea
When the awful chase commenced
And Parson B began to run
His lovely lame last wife
La Ultima
To ground.

Lame?
Oh yes!
She limped, poor thing
Crippled
But also young and beautiful
If a bit kittenish.
"Luscious,"
My George called her.
He said her limp
Made her seem more desirable
That it was kind of sexy.
I know what he means
I think
God knows that she was there
To be plucked but
Not because of her limp.
No
No one could have outrun
What was coming.
Gertie said it started with screams
Horrible screams
And pleadings
Poor woman was trying to flee.
"No, Matthew
"Oh my God, don't!"
"Matthew" being Matthew Baker
Our Parson B.
"No, no, no, oh my God!"
Gertie couldn't see it,

Fanny

She'd stayed put
Shaking
Shaking in her big old
Immaculate white shoes
Alone in the kitchen
With her forgotten tea
And two of those cookies
Shaped like seashells
She calls "madda-lanes."
She could not see our Parson B
Stalking the Luscious Limper
Room to room
But she could hear.
Hear screams
And shots . . .
Shots?
Oh yes
Shooting!
Parson B firing his big old pistol
At his lovely young wife.
Our Parson B for Lord's sake
Blasting away
Like macaroni western.
Blam tinkle crash
Oh oh, that one whacked the
Huge chandelier of Czechoslovak glass
In the Bakers' green dining room
Cutting graceful strands of
Crystal that late afternoon sun

Flowing through tall windows
Had turned to jewels
As they rained down
On Duncan Phyfe—
The long three-pedestal
Dining room table with
Inlaid border of golden wood—
Coming to rest on blue
Aubusson rug beneath.
Bang blam plish!
Now he's hit The Limper's arm
There, right there, forearm.
Only a nick but huge screams
Well I'd scream too.
She's moving faster now
Blam!
Slick as a whistle
This one blew the head off
Chinese dog with almond eyes
That sat on ocean side
Of marble hearth.
What was that dog called?
. . . Staff?
Staffordshire, that's it!
Sappy looking
Staffordshire china dog.
Plunk-zing
Now he's dinged antique brass andirons
From long ago Baker

Fanny

Family plantation in South Carolina
Setting off high-pitched ricochet whine.
Blam pop, pop, plish!
Oh, oh,
He's hit her lame leg
No ricochet there
No, no,
Slug stayed put.
She's screaming now
Screaming from a crawl.
Well, who wouldn't?
Yes screaming and crawling
And drenched in blood
As wicked wretch
In round collar staggers after.
Well,
Gertie back in kitchen
Is standing now
On her two feet
Standing, shaking
Like unbalanced washing machine.
Standing behind
Her old white kitchen chair
That she holds in death grip.
She's looking from kitchen
To the butler's pantry,
Looking at two swinging doors
Connecting butler's pantry
To dining room.

Door on right for
Taking food into dining room.
Door on left for
What comes back to kitchen.
Doors designed like that
To avoid staff collisions.
But Gertie is entire serving staff now
No one left to run into.
So she's just shaking by herself
And certainly not drinking tea.
She's terrified is what she is.
Collision that she fears
Is with Parson B
And his pistol
Barging in from dining room
Through butler's pantry to kitchen
Not necessarily through proper door . . .
Of course by now
If he did come
It would not matter what door he used
But Gertie said she did think
About rules on doors.
Well I'd have slumped in my teacup.

But not later
No No
Later I made Gertie tell all
Everything!
In time and rooms

Fanny

Through the house
Each scream, each crash
Each pistol shot.
She said the thing
Went on and on
Until at last
He shot her face
And that did kill her.
But even then
Not over
More, there was more.
Our Parson reloaded
And trudged upstairs,
Upstairs to second floor
Then to balcony off
Master bedroom
Balcony overlooking big fish pond
Balcony with that gorgeous view
Mountains so close
You can touch 'em.
That's when Our Parson put
Big old pistol into his mouth
And with one shot
Blew off his head
Well, top of it,
Lid of brain box
You might say,
Awful Awful.
Gun in mouth that tasted

My Food.
After that there was
Nothing for him to do
But to topple over into
Fish pond below
Fish pond that's home to ugly fish
Those gigantic foreign things . . .
What are they called?
Well fish
Yes fish for sure
Red
Orangie red
Orangie red revolting fish . . .
Japanese . . .
Carp!
Ugly devils!
They are carp!
By the time coroners had fished him out
Gertie said
Carp were dining
On fresh Parson. . . .
See it all in movie
You'd have to laugh
Hilarious
How could dumb movie-makers
Think audience would swallow all that
Even without carp?
But this was life
Not a movie

Fanny

And not funny in life
No not at all.
Both Bakers dead
Beautiful home looking like slaughterhouse
Rich blue Aubusson
Now soaked in blood
Czech chandelier in tatters. . . .
Oh and Georgian urn
He'd shot the urn
Lovely silver Georgian
Tea urn.
How many times did I
Help Gertie at big teas
When that gorgeous urn
Was used for pouring!
Now it's got extra outlets
To go with proper spigot and
Handle of fluted bone.
Not that it matters,
Who would use leaky urn now?
Certainly not Bakers
No they're gone
No need for tea
Not now.
Gunfire also smashed Chinese . . .
Chinese some kind of china
Dishes, cups and saucers . . .
Mrs. P's breakfront
Is full of it too, ex . . . expert?

No. . . Port . . . Export, that's it!
Chinese Export China. . . .
Oh and wallpaper
Our Parson got that wallpaper too
Special wallpaper . . .
What does Everett call that wallpaper . . .
Forget for minute . . .
It'll come to me . . .

Learned a lot from Everett
That bad boy nephew of mine.
Smart, he's smart,
Knows all about furniture,
Silver, beautiful things.
Swishy, no question, but I love him.
Everett will tell you:
Fanny got him started . . .
No, no, not that.
On beautiful things
What he calls Decorative Arts.
When he was little
His mother, my sister
Would leave him with me sometimes.
And if the Pearces were away
I'd let him wander around here alone.
Our Mansion is just as elegant as Bakers',
Even more
Yes more.
Here Everett was always serious

Fanny

He'd walk through Our Main Rooms
Quiet as a cat
Looking learning
Rubbing up against it all
Sniffing the air scented
With furniture polish and wax
Getting the feel of good stuff
Old things
Oriental rugs
Rare china
Paintings by famous artists.
Developing his eye he was.
Oh yes
He was marinated in the best juices
The very best.
And he did learn
One day when Pearces were gone
He was wandering through
Our downstairs public rooms
Gawking, soaking
Suddenly I hear familiar voice
"Oh, hello Everett, you startled me."
"I'm sorry, Mrs. Pearce,
"I thought you were away.
"I came to study your beautiful things."
"You did?"
Before I could retrieve him
She was giving him guided tour,
Main rooms, upstairs,

Walk-in vault in basement,
You name it.
Telling him correct names of things
Where they came from
Which ancestors had owned them
If any had
When she'd bought others
On which trip to Europe or Orient
Even bragged a bit about
Bargains picked up at auctions.
And that
As My George would say
Was when the "cement set up"
For Everett.
It was the beginning for him.
As a decorator yes,
But more, as a person,
A person-who's-found-what-interests-him.
He'd discovered what he wanted
To do with his life.
After that
With exception of the other thing
He changed completely.
He'd never studied in school before
Now he started,
Not only studying
But getting good grades.
Not just good
But very good.

Fanny

When high school was over
Mrs. P paid for university
Everett got degree in Art History.
Became interior decorator
He doesn't call it that . . .
No,
"Interior Design" he calls it.
By any name
It all goes to show
You never know
About people
Or life
Do you?
Like with Parson B
But different
Very different.
Everett went from pimply little darling
Prancing around like silly goose
To serious success story.
Now he's famous . . .
Well, let's just say
He's in demand
As a designer.
Does big places
Places owned by Old Money
People he met through the Pearces.
But now he has his own clients
And designs interiors for New Rich,
Homes of those seen lounging

In society pages
Fashion magazines
And even yellow tabloids,
Sorry to say.
But like I said
Everett's taught me a lot
About the Decorative Arts
Take the Bakers' wallpaper
I couldn't remember a bit ago,
Wallpaper on Parson's
Grocery list of gore.
Well it's Zoo . . . ugh, lost it again . . .
Wait, now it's coming back
Zoo , Zoo . . .
Receiving true name of wallpaper
Plugged by Our Parson
On his murderous trudge
Through his own home . . .
It's Zoob . . . Zuber, by god!
Wallpaper's Zuber!
France, French, comes from France,
Country scenes
People in funny clothes on horses.
Yes
Our Parson plugged Zuber too
Two slugs and lots of blood
All over fox hunting scene
In rolling country.
Hounds, horses

Fanny

And cute little red fox
Running for life he never loses
Because Zuber ends at moulding
In corner of room.
Before dogs can catch him
To tear his skinny little body to pieces
And brave men and
Women pursuing him—
Yes women too—
In red coats, white pants, top hats,
Black boots with wide
Tan band at top,
Before they can
Blow brass horns
To celebrate
The small thing's death,
Chop off its bushy tail
And make a toast.

In that very same entry hall
Gertie found the severed
Claw-on-ball foot
That Parson Baker had shot off
Antique Queen Anne chair
Causing chair to lean like Italian tower.
Gertie, my friend Gertie,
Ever the tidy one,
Slipped detached foot back
Under its leg of chair

Just to even things up
For now. . . .
When Benny Merkenburg
Our idiot Sheriff
Arrived to tie up loose ends of
One murder he could maybe solve
He pawed through his
Thimble-sized mind
To look for tips from TV shows.
"Take some notes
"They always take some notes."
Smoothing out his greasy
Napkin from lunch at
Dolly's Dockside Diner
Down by the harbor
He moistens pencil stub
With hunk of liver he calls a tongue
And aims his gigantic
Butt at Queen Anne
To pause on her to ponder
What to write.
Whoosh!
Her Majesty's foot shoots
Across the entry hall once more
And Benny is pitched onto floor.
Woulda paid to see it!

Anyhow
Getting all that from Gertie

Fanny

Took most of my day off
But I still had time to pump Manuel.
He knew the men
Who cleaned up after Parson Baker
"Sangre, sangre, sangre," Manuel said
Flesh too.
Manuel said gobs of Luscious Limper
Removed by Parson B's bullets
Ended up in strange places,
Vases and open drawers,
Behind picture frames.
Finger, her finger
One of the great marksman's
Shots took off a finger that
Landed in the open drawer
Of telephone table.
 Awful, awful
Amazing too:
Who left that drawer open?
How did they know?
Must be honest,
It is interesting
Details are gripping
In grisly way of course,
Fascinating
In a sick sense,
Awful
Bloody
Gory.

But as for me
When listening to how
Our Parson's shots moved
Bits of poor Mrs. B about and
Where they landed
Just plain "finger" wasn't enough.
Oh no.
"Which one, Manuel?" I say.
"Que?" says Manuel.
"Which finger got blown off ?"
I ask
Holding up my hand and
Wiggling fingers.
"No say," says Manuel
Clapping on his hat and leaving.
Think I embarrassed him.
But What If It Had Been Her Ring Finger!
Now that would be something
Her ring finger
Finger with diamond
That would choke a goat
Ring that would have been mine
If I'd accepted Parson B. . . .
Hope it didn't hurt diamond . . .
Not that it makes any difference now. . . .
Later Manuel admitted
That Mrs. P asked him everything too
Just like I did
In a more genteel

Fanny

Roundabout way of course.
Does that make me feel better?
I don't know
But it shows
Mrs. P's same as rest of us
When it comes to Morbid Fascination.
Doesn't it?

And I think that's one reason Mrs. P
Invites Mrs. L to come here so often:
Curiosity sparked by Morbid Fascination.
She wants to see
How steep the pitch
Has become for her friend
That's what I think.
Mrs. P's not being mean
No
Just human
Like the rest of us.
And she has more reasons
Besides Morbid Fascination.
Honest affection for her friend;
And never forget Time
Passage of time
Hankerings and highlights that brings,
Friends for so long
Fifty, sixty years, since childhood
Neighbors when they were little
Classmates from grade school on

Bridesmaids in weddings of others
And in their own.
Oh yes.
Been through so much together
Wars that took lovers
Classmates, kin, friends.
Illness, deaths, hard times, births
Everything that happened here
Right here
In this old house
Our Mansion:
Our Cammie's birth and
Tragedy of her condition
All the problems that's caused.
Poor Morgan Pearce's
Sickness and death
On and on and on.
Now they're old and shrinking up
Less and less of them to feed
Every day.
Moving slower
Maybe thinking slower
But their memory worlds
Are not slower.
They are running wild
Stuff is popping into their heads
For no reason
Old happenings
People looking just as they did

Fanny

When world was young
Faces arriving unasked
Out of order
All clamoring for attention . . .
Very mysterious
Why this person now
Why that day or event
After all these years?
Forgotten tunes
Words first heard
When Hector was a pup.
Enemies dead ages ago
Missed opportunities,
Secret, mercifully ungratified desires. . . .
Oh yes
After all these years their
Dancers are still dancing,
Alive to them
To them alone.

Like I said,
Mrs. L had very bright mind.
Successful business woman she was,
Real estate
Big properties in City
And out here too.
Clever
Quicker that way than Mrs. P
Specially with numbers

And business chitchat
Had her own agency.
Oh yes
Brokering, buying, selling,
For others and herself
Good training for her tongue
No doubt.
"Here comes the scarred
"Survivor of the realtor wars"
Mr. P would mumble,
Walking away quickly.
Oh yes, no doubt
But she was a natural.
Probably made canny chinwag
In bassinet,
Born clutching tricky handbag
And never stopped learning new ones.
Take her dangling sentences:
First comes charm and
Rapid fire delivery
Busy ha-ha chatter
To dazzle and to lull
Make other person feel easy;
Next comes sudden stop
Or gentle fade
Take your choice
Either way delivery stops;
Throw in wave of hand
Or nod

Fanny

As if saying
"You know the tune,
"You finish song."
But it ain't song
It's trap.
Mrs. L waits
Patiently waits
Maybe hums old show tune
While wandering around
Like her mind is on vacation.
She's just jigging the bait
To tempt the mullet
To bite on her baited
Broken sentence
A little pause
While silence does its work.
Then client can no longer stand suspense
Strikes the bait and swallows hook
Finishing Mrs. L's sentence
With her own thought or wish.
Now Mrs. L knows client's mind.
Sets hook and drags client
Up steps
And through front door,
Into contract.
It's all a kind of art
Not exalted art of course
But still an art.
Mrs. L has that gift.

Not so simple
Must have patience
And ear for it,
Rhythm, timing.
In her prime she was past master
Now
Time passing
She may be failing.
Or is she?

And that mystery rivets Mrs. P,
Drawing her to the question of
Her brilliant friend's condition
Like cat is to old fish wrappings.
Transfixed she is
By Mrs. L's slide
Into the dotty bag
If she is so sliding,
That is my thought.
Mrs. P cannot help herself.
Last embers of some old rivalry?
Perhaps.
More likely she's thinking,
"If that could happen to Gladys . . .
"Why that could happen to me too!"
I don't know
But like I said before
The one I really wonder about
Is Mrs. L.

Fanny

What does Mrs. L think?
Does she see Mrs. P's morbid stare?
Does she resent it?
If she does
Why sure
You might say, sure,
She could resent
Mrs. P's attachment
To her condition.
Or take offense that Mrs. P invites her here
Then goes to wedding leaving her alone
With Cammie, Staff, and old movie. . . .
Or you might think
That's such a little thing
It would be petty of Mrs. L
To harbor hard feelings
About a small slight. . . .
But between old friends
Maybe not so small.
Beneath her calm acceptance
Mrs. L might resent demotion
From houseguest to babysitter
Despite her protest that it's just fine.
Would it be so surprising if she—
Especially at her age—
Should feel resentfulness
And stumble briefly back
To childhood fantasies
Of evening up the score?

But even if she held a grudge
What could she do?
She'd have to have sway
And she's got none
None.
Former hotshot realtor, wheeler-dealer
Old friend, houseguest
Yes,
But now she looks to be
Ditzy old lady:
No firm footing
No leverage.
What could she do?

Hold on Fanny
Wait a minute
Think again
Sway depends
It all depends
Weakest of us always has some
Some angle
Some place to stand
A narrow ledge
A fingerhold
To use for leverage,
What little leverage
We may command.
That can add up to sway.
Remember Yankee Windlass!

Fanny

Yankee Windlass My George
Raves about,
Recipe for leverage in real world.
Never seen a real one
But they exist
Oh yes
And do amazing things
Can move mountains
George said.
He made one here,
Right here in My Kitchen
Working model
Out of chopsticks, string and
A bit of his duct tape.
First he made a cross
With two chopsticks,
And stuck the bottom of vertical one
In the hole in our
Heavy old cutting board
To keep the chopstick standing straight—
Like mast of boat—
Then he tied piece of string
To top of our pepper grinder,
Wrapped other end
Around straight-up chopstick
And cranked on crosspiece
So that the string wound up
On the straight-up chopstick.
And that finally pulled the grinder over.

My George said that
If he had real Yankee Windlass
Big one of course
He could topple this whole house
Our Mansion
God forbid.
All by himself,
If he had enough line,
Cable he said,
Attached to upper part of house.
Oh, and mule would help
Pickup, tractor even better . . .
Going round and round the post
Winding the cable up . . .
In tiny bites
Slow and easy.
Enough of that
George said
And little by little
This whole house would come loose
And rise from its foundations
Topple over.
All make-believe of course
But made awful picture
Terrifying, apocalypse
Destruction of Our Mansion
Beautiful house
My Kitchen
My Two Light Rooms

Fanny

And sounds
Imagine sounds.
Creaks at first
Then snaps and pops
Heart-rending groans
Finally loud explosions
As it all leaves foundations.
Our World at sea
Tipping and rocking
Swaying, tilting, cockeyed.
House rolling over
Back edge of flat floor rising
Contents of house sliding
Sliding down toward meadow-side walls
Like Manuel emptying wheelbarrow.
Front walls now lying
Right on ground.
Everything drawn toward My George
Way down there in Lower Meadow
Cranking away on his
Crazy Yankee Windlass.
Back walls now ceilings
Pictures hanging down like
My George's plumb bobs.
Stuff sliding off sideboard
Bureaus, tables.
Vases smashed
Flowers freed
Floating on puddled floor

That recently was wall.
Crazy house
All because of Miracle of Leverage
And mysterious power of Yankee Windlass.
In Living Room
Antiques are breaking up.
In My Kitchen,
My Two Nice Light Rooms
Things are crashing
Through meadow-side windows.
My Stove, My TV . . .
And what about Me!
Running to save my life
Door's on the floor
Opens on dirt.
I'm shouting at My George
But can't find way out
Telling him to
"Quit cranking on your damn
"Yankee Windlass!"
As if,
Way down in Lower Meadow,
He could hear me!
Waking nightmare
Silly fantasy.
But I say that in life
It's the same with sway:
Sway is power.
What if Mrs. L remembers

Fanny

Remembers what happened with Cammie
But forgets it can't be mentioned?
Or she doesn't forget
But tells Cammie anyway?
Sway by mistake
Sway on purpose
She's got sway either way
Power to change things
For better or worse.
Does Mrs. L remember
What she and Mrs. P decided
For Cammie long ago?
For Cammie's good of course.
Because if Mrs. L does remember
She might let it out
No question
She might.
Maybe without thinking
Just in chatting
By mistake,
A weak moment
Just to see what happens,
One way or another . . .
Could easily let it out
That's my fear.

So when,
A little bit ago
From My Kitchen window,

I saw Cammie going
To Rose Garden
I hurried to the Library
To remind Mrs. L
Not to talk to Cammie
About "back then,"
Or Her Harvey,
And definitely not about weddings.
But now I'm wondering . . .
Did my Good Intentions
Set a trap for myself?
I meant well warning Mrs. L
What not to talk about,
But Good Intentions no guarantee.
No
Sometimes happens
The other way around.
Like that night with My George,
Cat Serious and Mouse.
George and I were snuggling,
Warming up to the liquid ritual
When My Cat Serious appears on
The porch outside our room
To offer entertainment.
Serious has top billing,
Mouse—hanging from corner
Of her mouth like soggy butt
In Humphrey Bogart flick—
Is straight man.

Fanny

As we all know
Cats love dragging their trophies home.
This one has added allure
Of being alive, squeaking,
And in general
Behaving as if wishing
To continue life unopened.
Mouse can easily imagine
Where all this is headed . . .
What?
Oh all right
If not actually imagine
Have a clear
Sense of an ending.
But wait!
Now comes My George!
Drunk with rage
At the prospect
Of a murder on the stage.
He leaps o'er the apron
To the boards
Forgetting me,
And our date in the Garden of Love. . . .
I must say
Men are funny . . .
"Nuts" would not be
Too strong a word.
Imagine
Just imagine

My George was demanding
That Cat Serious show . . .
What? Sensitivity?
Christian charity?
"George," I say,
"For God's sake, George,
"It's what cats do,
"Cats kill things."
"Shit," says My George. "Not OK!
"This ain't killing, it's torture!
"That Mouse is still alive!"
"George," I say.
"That Mouse means as much to Serious
"As an old fan belt does to you:
"Trash already."
"It's torture!"
"Right George
"But cats do that too
"And Serious is cat."
"Ahrrrgg!" says My George
Kicking off the bedclothes
And barging through screen door
Out onto porch shouting,
"I'm kicking bloody cat
"Between bloody uprights!"
This sudden male fury
Shocks Serious.
She takes one look
At naked lunatic

Fanny

Leaping onto Her Porch
Cake falling,
Huge foot cocked . . .
She flies,
As cats can do
Porch to roof to sheltering night.
But not before she's dropped
The Mouse
Where George's foot must fall.
So George
Full of misplaced morals,
Careening like runaway train,
Puts end to torture of the Mouse
As well as to the Mouse itself.
Then
Back from his failed rescue mission
With squashed mouse oozing up
Between finger-sized toes,
He bounces into the bathroom
On clean foot while
Holding murderous one aloft,
Hops to toilet to flush
Remains of flattened mouse down drain,
Then sits
On edge of tub,
Muttering as he washes feet.
I laughed
Oh how I laughed . . .
Sex is great

But laughter lasts longer.

Now,
Recalling My George's Good Intentions
Towards The Mouse—
If you can call them that—
And how they did not save it,
I worry that my warning to Mrs. L
May only have reminded her
Of what she should not say
Making it more likely
That by mistake
Or out of pique,
She would say it.
At first I thought
I'd seen no sign
Of anything that might
Trigger her resentment
Until I remembered that,
On that very afternoon—
Bugles blaring, flags waving—
Mrs. P's regimental side
Had galloped up to muster and dispatch
Her golf cart train
To the Weldon Wedding,
Organizing it so as to freeze out Mrs. L
And deprive her
Of the high point of her weekend.
Reminding me

Fanny

That Mrs. P has always been
A bit of a puppet master
Thriving on ordering others about,
For their own good, of course.
Long ago
Before the children had grown up
People got about Our Estate
In donkey carts
Outfitted with bud vases,
Embroidered seat cushions and
Black Watch lap robes.
Before we went to golf carts,
Before the donkeys had moved on
Taking their hee-haws, clip-clops
And fragrant droppings with them,
Back then
Even back then
On occasions like this
Mr. P would look toward Mrs. P,
And mutter,
"She should have been a theater director . . ."
"Well," I say,
"Forget theater director:
"She is THE Director
"Director of Other People's Lives."
And I wonder if,
After all these years,
Mightn't someone,
Mrs. L in her dotage—

Cammie in her damage—
Have become tired
Of being ordered about?

Be that
As it might someday be,
This afternoon when Mrs. P
Took command on
The Upper Lawn
The guests all smiled politely
And said things like,
"This is so exciting
"Riding in golf carts to wedding"
When what they really want to do
Is to go in their own big cars.
Or better yet
Lie down to let my delicious
Midday dinner settle
And to hell with wedding.
Of course
What they should do is walk,
A glance will tell you that,
But none can escape Mrs. P.
So they get in the carts
Except for Mrs. L.
Why didn't Mrs. P just tell the Weldons
That she's bringing her houseguest Mrs. L,
They've known Mrs. L forever?
For that matter

Fanny

Why did Mrs. P invite Mrs. L to stay
When she knew they'd all be
Going to a wedding
Where Mrs. L is not invited?
I think I know.
I think Mrs. P has had a plan all along,
A plan she did not want to talk about,
A plan for something practical,
Yes!
Like babysitting!
That's what I think.
I think Mrs. P is worried
About leaving Cammie here
To watch a wedding on TV
When Cammie knows
That everyone here is going
To a real one.
It's risky
Considering Cammie's love-hate feelings
About weddings.
So Mrs. P decides
That someone who Cammie knows well,
Like Mrs. L,
Should remain here with her.
Me?
I'm babysitter to the babysitter
Well that's OK with me.
But it was sad to see
Our Cammie on the Upper Lawn

As her mother and the houseguests
Climbed into carts.
Mrs. P whispered to Mrs. L
"Will you be all right? "
Meaning will Mrs. L be all right
While everyone else has gone to wedding.
"Oh yes, Irene, thank you dear
"After that lovely meal of Fanny's
"I just want to watch that
"That wonderful movie
"In your beautiful library,"
Agreeing to what
Can't be changed anyway.
"Can I, can I?" Cammie says softly,
Being the only one who really wants
To go to the wedding
Fascinated with them like she is.
"No Cammie dear
"There's not enough room,"
Says her mother.
"Let her have my place, Irene,"
Says Mr. Sterling.
"No, no, sit down, John!
"Please sit down."
Says Mrs. P
Ready to kill him.
"I need your advice on the way,
"About planting by the Great Lake."
Well, believe me,

Fanny

Mr. Sterling is a banker
Never held a trowel in his hand
Let alone a handful of dirt
Doesn't know rose from rhododendron
Beautiful garden at his place
But all gardening done by crew,
Friends of Manuel's.
So once again
Our Cammie is the casualty.
She walks slowly over the lawn
Back into Our Mansion
As Mrs. L says to Mrs. P
"I'll just go in and sit with her dear"
And scurries off into Our Mansion too.
"Oh, thank you dear," says Mrs. P.
Pretending that never occurred to her.

Then Mrs. P sitting in the first cart
Raises her hand
Waves it in a circle
Like John Wayne as
The captain of big cattle drive.
The carts groan, creak and
Begin to snake their way
Along the winding path
Toward The Meadow far below,
Where the path disappears in trees
And the mountains surge up
Suddenly like a wall.

The women in bright spring dresses
And floppy hats
Laugh and point to where
The men should look.
The men nod and obey.
Down through lush gardens
Gently dropping from terrace to terrace
Beside the creek whose little waterfalls
Trickle musically into oval pools
Each one lower
And larger than the last
Until the watery staircase
Falls into the last pool
That lies across the foot
Of The Meadow
A great green oval lake
Where frogs and fishes hide
Under water lilies before
Becoming supper for
The two blue heron
That fly up from the shore
Each evening at dusk.
For us left standing
On the Upper Lawn
It's a scene from one of
Those Italian films.
The crazy little train of carts
Like a gypsy circus
Striped canopies and chattering cargo

Fanny

Getting smaller and smaller 'til
They vanish in the trees
At Meadow's end
And are gone
All gone.

Back in Our Mansion
I hear Mrs. L talking
To Cammie in Library
"Oh Cammie . . .
"Cammie Cammie Cammie . . .
"You were such an adorable child!
"And beautiful young woman too!
"So gorgeous at your sister's wedding.
"Such a lovely maid-of-honor
"So tan and calm,
"That gorgeous aqua dress.
"Their wedding came at a hard time
"For you I know
"And I never understood . . .
"Your mother is my dearest friend
"But I could never understand. . ."
Then I can't hear more
Well I'm shaken
That old lady knows
Or should know
Better than me
What happened
Has she forgotten?

So I go down the hall
To look through the Library doors.
They're sitting with their backs to me
Mrs. L is silent, reading "Vogue."
Cammie's facing TV
Saying nothing
Flipping cards on her little table
No sign she even heard Mrs. L.
But I know Our Cammie
Seen it often
She hears
But does not show.
So like I said before
I decide I must say
Something to Mrs. L
When she's alone
To remind her to be careful
What she says to Cammie
About The Past.

Why,
Even to me
It seems like only yesterday
Think how real it must seem
To Our Cammie
Even if she isn't all there.
Saturday
It was a Saturday in May
The Russells

Fanny

Parents of Cammie's Harvey
Were coming here
They'd asked to meet with Pearces
Did not say why.
Pearces and Russells knew each other
Not close
But on good terms,
They had kids
With similar problems.
So Mrs. P invited the Russells
To informal Luncheon here
Outside
On patio off Upper Lawn
Where great clusters of wisteria
Cascade down the walls.
The plan was for
Cammie and Harvey to go
To the Olive Orchard
The little Greek restaurant,
More like roadhouse really,
Which Cammie and Harvey loved.
Edgar, Harvey's caregiver would drive.
He'd eat in the Tap Room
Watching TV, baseball or whatever
While Cammie and Harvey
Would sit in their own booth
For lunch all by themselves.
Meanwhile the . . .
I almost said, "grownups" . . .

The Russells and the Pearces
Would be here at Our House
Enjoying the Luncheon
Luncheon Old Cook and I prepared.
The big day when it came
Was beautiful and the night was
Going to be full moon.
I had night off
Meeting My George I was.
Lovely summer
What a lovely summer that was. . . .
The air was soft and sweet
With summer smells
Especially jasmine
With its lazy sexy perfume.
I was happy, so happy
Just like Cammie
When you're young. . . .
But first I had to help Old Cook
Make special Luncheon
For the Parents.
We wanted to do Our Cammie proud
She'd fallen in love.
True she wasn't all there
But even if not one hundred percent
In certain departments
She was a girl.
And beautiful then too
Beautiful . . .

Fanny

Also, yes,
Appealing, very appealing.
Why couldn't she fall in love
Like anybody else?
Like me and My George?
Like the Pearces,
If they ever did . . .
Like any of us?
It's all so long ago
All those years gone by now
And for what came after . . .
Nothing you'd ever want
To cause Cammie to remember.
So,
Like I said before,
Today when I saw Cammie start
Her regular little Rose Garden walk
Before time for their movie
I hurried over to the Library
To tell Mrs. L not to talk to Cammie
About what happened long ago
About Harvey
And so forth.
I've known Mrs. L so long
I know her almost as well
As I know Mrs. P.
I can talk to her about anything
Including family stuff.
"You know Mrs. Lloyd

"We have to be careful
"Careful about what we say
"To Cammie
"Even after all these years."
Mrs. L says right away
"Oh my, Fanny
"You don't have to remind me about that!"
So I think
OK good,
She knows what I'm talking about.
There's this little pause and she says
"But what exactly do you mean?"
"About weddings" I say
"About weddings" she says
Nodding her head firmly
That makes me think again
That she's on track
Understands me.
"Yes Mrs. Lloyd you know
"Weddings remind Cammie of Harvey.
"You remember Harvey don't you?"
"Oh of course," she says.
Another pause
"But which Harvey do you mean?"
"Why you know as well as I do,
"I mean Cammie's Harvey."
"Yes?"
Is all she says
Like I'm supposed to go on

Fanny

I turn around to check
But no Cammie
Not back from her walk yet.
"Mrs. Lloyd you were here that Saturday
"When Harvey's parents,
"The Russells, came for lunch."
"Oh Fanny, what a beautiful lunch!"
Well I'm always grateful for thanks
Even about a long ago meal
And one made mostly by Old Cook
Besides it shows Mrs. L's registering.
But then she says
"Where did you ever
"Find such delicious raspberries?"
And I realize she's thinking
Of lunch today
"No no not today Mrs. Lloyd!
"Not today!"
I'm starting to lose patience
My George has warned me about that
But what the hell
No time to waste
Cammie may come back any minute.
"Look Mrs. Lloyd you remember
"What Harvey's parents offered
"Don't you?"
In middle of my saying that
The Old Lady starts doing strange things
Rolls her eyes

Waves her hands
Then brings hands together
In praying position.
"Mrs. Lloyd think
"Think back
"Harvey's parents, the Russells,
"They said they knew
"And that everyone knew
"Cammie and Harvey were in love."
Now Mrs. L is puckering her lips
Uttering little "ooooohs" and "aaaahhhs"
I say to myself oh oh
She's losing it
I must hurry
It's my last chance.
"Harvey's parents Mrs. Lloyd
"Remember how they offered to get
Harvey fixed and . . ."
"Fixed up?
"Oh yes, yes, I remember that"
Nodding her head while shaking it.
"No no" Mrs. Lloyd
"Fixed!"
"You know
"So the marriage
"Could not lead to children
"And after the operation
"Cammie and Harvey could get married
"The Russells would give them

Fanny

"That cottage on their estate to live in."
"Ooooh no Fanny no!"
The Old Lady says
Putting hands over ears.
Oh yes
That's what she does
Opens eyes soup bowl size
With her droopy eyelids
Takes major effort.
"Mrs. Lloyd
"The Russells said they had 'explored'
"The idea of a wedding with Harvey
"Whatever 'explored' meant
"And they knew Harvey cared
"Very much for Cammie
"They also said that
"Of course
"They hadn't said anything to Harvey
"Or to Cammie
"About the 'getting fixed' part."
Well in the middle of my saying all that
Mrs. L pulls her lips inside her mouth
Squeezes her eyes shut tight
Hands over ears.
I keep right on,
"Mrs. Lloyd
"Remember how Mr. Pearce said
"He thought the Russell's plan
"Was an excellent idea?

"He was all for letting them be married,
"Said that it would make them happy
"And their marriage
"After Harvey's operation
"Should not cause any problems
"Such as children.
"Remember Mrs. Lloyd?
"And how right away Mrs. P said
"She did not think it was a good idea
"Not at all.
"In fact she let the Russells know
"In no uncertain terms
"It wasn't going to happen
"There would be no wedding.
"And that was the end
"Of the Luncheon.
"Mr. Russell called Edgar
"At the Olive Orchard
"Edgar brought Cammie here
"And Cammie and Harvey
"Never saw each other again.
"A few months later Harvey turned up
"Face down in Russell's swimming pool
"Drowned dead.
"Mrs. L,
"Cammie still doesn't know
"About that
"She still doesn't know
"What happened to Her Harvey."

Fanny

Well, I'm about to speak even louder
But I get an awful feeling in my stomach
I turn around
And there she is.
Cammie
Sitting at her little table
Dealing solitaire.
She'd come back in behind me
While I was lecturing Mrs. L.
When?
When did she do that?
When did she return
From the Rose Garden?
What did she hear?
Why didn't Mrs. L tell me?
Give me a sign?
Was that what all her faces were about?
I don't know
I do not know.

Now Mrs. L
Can say to Mrs. P
"I tried to tell Fanny
"Tried to warn her
"Tried to let her know
"That Cammie had come back in
"I did everything
"But pound my head on the table."
Yes Mrs. L

You did everything
But simply say
"Hello Cammie"
Why didn't she just say
"Hello Cammie."
Well, by then there was
Nothing more to be done
Or said to Mrs. L or anyone.
And by then it's time
For their movie
So I say
"Time for Princess Grace"
"Oh good" says Mrs. L
Opening her eyes and coming alive.
Credits for "High Society" begin
And I escape.

The movie's been on now
For about an hour
Over there in the Library.
Mrs. L and Cammie watching
Beautiful Princess Grace
And Bing Crosby and Louis Armstrong
As Manuel's big fire snaps and pops
While I've been here
Stewing in my tea.
You're holding bag Fanny
If something happens on this one
You're holding bag.

Fanny

Now Mrs. L can say
To Mrs. P
"Oh Irene, Fanny told Cammie
"Not directly of course
"No no
"I'm sure Fanny had best intentions
"But she was talking
"In front of Cammie
"About that whole sad affair
"You know
"The Russells' idea about how
"How Cammie and Harvey might marry
"After they'd given Harvey his operation . . .
"That unusual idea
"We've never mentioned since.
"Fanny went into all that
"With Camilla sitting right there
"Oh yes
"She did
"And with me trying to stop her
"But I couldn't stop her."
What'll I say to that?
"Mrs. L your dotty friend
"Was doing it all by herself.
"She brought it up to Cammie
"And I was just trying
"To shut her up . . .
"I never saw Cammie come in and
"Mrs. L. never let me know

"She'd come back."
But I won't say that
Wouldn't do any good if I did.

Later
On that beautiful Saturday,
After Harvey's parents had gone,
I heard Mrs. P talking to Mr. P:
"Disgusting! Absolutely disgusting.
"Treating those children
"As if they're animals."
Mr. P said it seemed to him
Like a decent solution.
He pointed out in his quiet way
That they weren't children in their bodies.
"That's just the point," she said.
Which is her way
Of turning things upside down.
Mr. P tried to protest
And defend Harvey's parents' idea
But he'd lost the argument
And he knew it.
She always got her way
And Mrs. P's way got support from Mrs. L.
Why were they so against it?
Of course it would have been unusual
And I can see that it might not
Have been as simple as it seems.
Could have been hard to explain.

Fanny

Two somewhat-less-than-normals
Living together, married actually.
Would have raised a lot of questions
I can see that
I suppose some eyebrows too.
My George wondered
Would it even be legal?
Could parents do that for a kid
Do that to a kid like Harvey?
Could Cammie and Harvey
Even get a marriage license?
I don't know
Not an "open and shut case"
As Mr. P used to say.
Surely would have been unusual.
But why did it make them so angry
Mrs. P and Mrs. L?
They could have said "no"
But were they really angry
Or just pretending?
Show of righteous indignation?
To keep up appearance
For the sake of old standards?
I would have thought
They'd want the young people
To have a life together.

Well
Old Cook, she knew.
"Consider appearances" she said.
"What it would have looked like;
"Talk, imagine talk
"Gossip at dinner parties
"Tittering over bridge
"After luncheon at Garden Club
"Country Club
"Golf
"During and after golf
"In the bar
"Locker room
"Smirking and giggling
"Especially Our Cammie
"Being so beautiful."
"With these people,"
Old Cook said.
"With anybody really,
"You have to consider appearances.
"Would not have looked good
"Not to their group,
"Others too I suppose."
"Would have seemed like
"Adults were arranging
"For children to play house for real.
"That really isn't done."

Fanny

Oh, oh, look at the clock!
Soon they'll all be back
From the wedding.
Time to lay out
Cold cuts, crackers
And the cheese.
The golf cart train will be
Climbing the winding path
Back to Our Mansion with
Mrs. P and our Houseguests
Who will have witnessed
Yet another Society wedding,
Gobbled more catered food
Greeted old friends
And avoided others
Gossiped
Held forth on favorite topics
And tippled to fight the boredom.
Well, God bless 'em,
That's their problem.
We'll spread out the cold food
Like I said but
There's the end of it.
It's understood between
Mrs. P and me
That after big days like today
My George and I will be
In charge.
Cammie will be full of

Her movie wedding and
Wanting to talk about it.
But she can't do that
With Our Houseguests.
No
That could never happen.
So she will come with us
Me and My George
To our, the Servants' Side;
She'll get the burger that she loves,
Ice cream, choice of topping,
George and I will have tea.
We'll all play cards,
Go Fish no doubt,
Which Cammie loves
Because with any luck
She gets to tell others
What to do,
As she's so often seen
Her mother do.
"Go Fish!" she tells My George
Giggles bursting
Or,
Straight face, stern voice,
"Now you can just Go fish
"For that George!"
Sometimes My George will bring
His banjo and we'll sing
Or he'll tell some silly story

Fanny

That she's heard for years but
Is always fresh for her.
Cammie loves these evenings
And so do we.
She talks a lot
Laughs easily,
Which is not always true these days,
That makes us happy too.
Later she will hold out bravely
But when she nods
And leans on me
Or takes my hand
I know it's time
For us to slip away
Up the back stairs
Over to the Family's Side
To her own room above
Our Main Rooms where
Mrs. P, Mrs. L
And Our Houseguests
Are putting their reviews
Of Their Wedding
Of My Luncheon
And of Their Day to bed.
Now
My George and I are free.
We'll grab our coats and pile into
His gleaming '32 Ford Phaeton
Go out for a beer

Listen to some music
Do some dancing . . .
Maybe stop by Slyde Inn
To get a draught
From tall Wee Em.
We've heard she has
A new love now
So we'll be spared
Her weepy tales about
Losing her head over
Richard-the-Chauffeur who
Of course then lost his own.

After Wee Em, we'll
Race home against the fog
As it slides in over the waves
Snug as a hatch cover
Snuffing the stars
And sending us to bed.
Now Cat Serious can raise hell
On the porch off our room
And we won't hear a thing.
Possums and cats and owls
Will own the night
And, needs must,
Our Estate in the Country.

JAMES WOOD, the author of *Fanny* and *Proust's Macaroon* practiced law in New York City and Los Angeles and worked at various jobs including tours at a think tank, as a section hand on the Alaska Railroad and as a roughneck in the oil fields. From time to time he returned to university to study art, medieval history, poetry, playwriting and directing.

CPSIA information can be obtained
at www.ICGtesting.com
Printed in the USA
BVHW080027041218
534638BV00010B/790/P